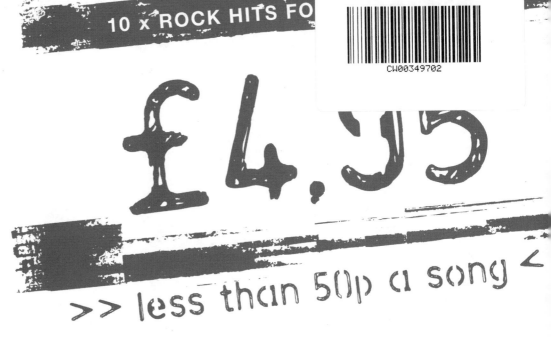

10 x ROCK HITS FO

£4.95

>> less than 50p a song <

10 x Ultimate Rock Hits

PVG

This publication is not authorised for sale in
the United States of America and / or Canada

WISE PUBLICATIONS
part of The Music Sales Group
London / New York / Paris / Sydney / Copenhagen / Berlin / Madrid / Tokyo

Published by
Wise Publications
8/9 Frith Street, London, W1D 3JB, England.

Exclusive distributors:
Music Sales Limited
Distribution Centre, Newmarket Road,
Bury St Edmunds, Suffolk, IP33 3YB, England.

Music Sales Pty Limited
120 Rothschild Avenue, Rosebery, NSW 2018, Australia.

Order No. AM985534
ISBN 1-84609-558-1

This book © Copyright 2006 Wise Publications,
a division of Music Sales Limited.

Unauthorised reproduction of any part of this publication by
any means including photocopying is an infringement of copyright.

Printed in the EU.

www.musicsales.com

Your Guarantee of Quality:
As publishers, we strive to produce every book
to the highest commercial standards.

The book has been carefully designed to minimise awkward page turns
and to make playing from it a real pleasure. Particular care has been given
to specifying acid-free, neutral-sized paper made from pulps
which have not been elemental chlorine bleached.

This pulp is from farmed sustainable forests and
was produced with special regard for the environment.

Throughout, the printing and binding have been planned
to ensure a sturdy, attractive publication which should give
years of enjoyment.

If your copy fails to meet our high standards, please inform us
and we will gladly replace it.

Bring Me To Life

Words & Music by Ben Moody, Amy Lee & David Hodges

1. (Female) How can you see into my eyes, like open doors? Leading you down

© Copyright 2003 Dwight Frye Music Incorporated, USA/Zombies Ate My Publishing/Forthfallen Publishing.
Universal/MCA Music Limited.
All Rights Reserved. International Copyright Secured.

8

Do You Want To

Words & Music by Alexander Kapranos, Nicholas McCarthy, Robert Hardy & Paul Thomson

© Copyright 2005 Universal Music Publishing Limited.
All Rights Reserved. International Copyright Secured.

To Coda ⊕

go { where what } (2. ℅) of I've ne-ver let__ you be-fore?__ (Doo doo doo, doo__

__ doo doo doo doo doo.)

Well, he's a friend and he's so proud of__ ya.
Well, he's a friend and we're so proud of__ ya.

1.

He's a friend and I knew him be-fore__ ya, oh yeah._____
Your fa-mous friend, well I (Doo doo doo, doo__

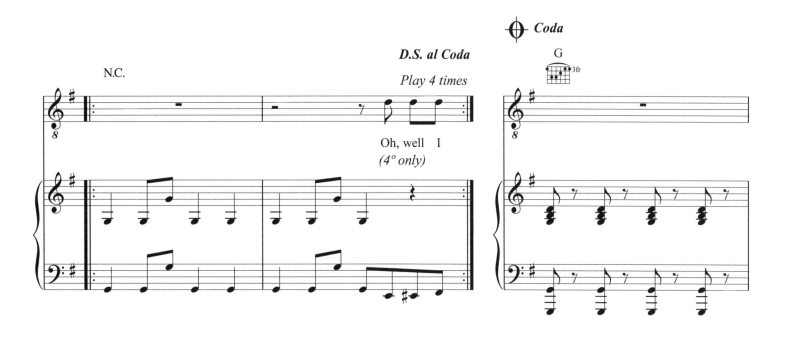

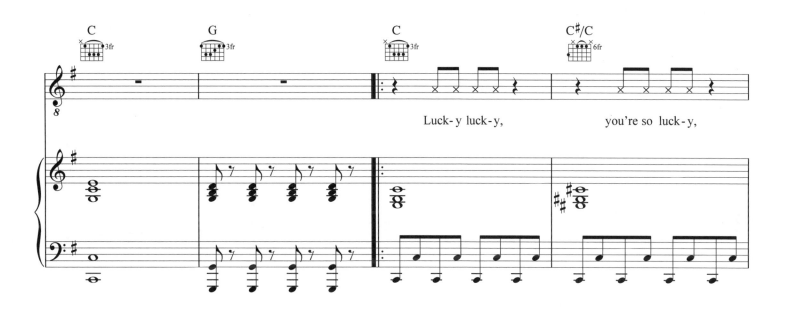

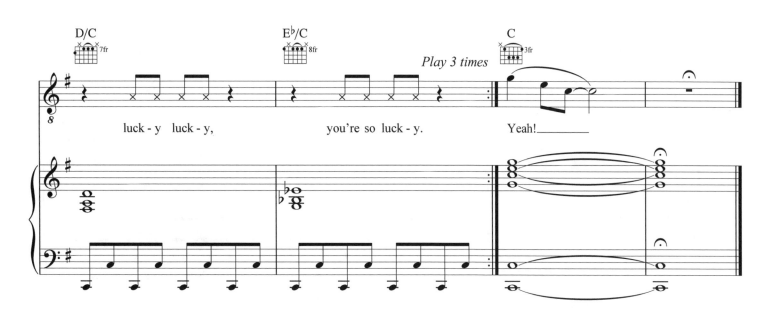

How Soon Is Now?

Words & Music by Morrissey & Johnny Marr

© Copyright 1984 Universal Music Publishing Limited (50%)/Copyright Control (50%).
All Rights Reserved. International Copyright Secured.

I am the

There's a club if you'd like to go, _____ you could meet some-bo-dy_____ who real-ly loves_ you. So you go and you stand on your own, and you leave on your own, and you go home and you cry and you want to die.___

Repeat and fade

19

I Predict A Riot

Words & Music by Nicholas Hodgson, Richard Wilson,
Andrew White, James Rix & Nicholas Baines

© Copyright 2004 Rondor Music (London) Limited.
All Rights Reserved. International Copyright Secured.

Cm

1. Oh, watch-ing the peo - ple get
2. Oh, I try to get___ to my

Eb   F   Cm

lai - ry is not ve - ry pret - ty, I tell thee.
ta - xi; a man in a track - suit at - tacks me, he

Eb   F

Walk-ing through town___ is quite sca - ry, and not ve - ry sen - si - ble
said that he saw___ it be - fore me, wants to get things___ a bit

Cm   Eb

ei - ther. A friend of a friend,___ he got beat - en, he
go - ry. Girls run a - round___ with no clothes on to
(𝄋) watch-ing the peo - ple get lai - ry is

21

looked the wrong way____ at a po - - liceman; would
bor - row a pound____ for a con - - dom; if it
not ve - ry pret - ty I tell thee.

ne - ver have hap - pened to Smea - - ton, an
was - n't for chip - fat they'd be fro - - zen. They're
Walk - ing through town____ is quite sca - - ry, and

old Le - o - den - si - an.
not ve - ry sen - si - ble.
not ve - ry sen - si - ble.
La,_____

Cigarettes & Alcohol

Words & Music by Noel Gallagher

1. Is it my—
(Verse 2 see block lyric)

© Copyright 1994 Creation Songs Limited/Oasis Music (GB).
Sony/ATV Music Publishing (UK) Limited.
All Rights Reserved. International Copyright Secured.

i - ma - gi - na - tion, or have I fi - nal - ly found— some-

- thing worth liv - ing for?——

I was look - ing for some ac -

- tion, but all— I found— was ci - gar - ettes and al - co - hol.—

You could wait for a life - time,

to spend your days in the sun - shine,

you might as well do the white—

line   'cos when it comes on top,—

you got - ta make it hap-

- pen,＿＿＿

you got - ta make it hap - pen,＿＿＿

you got - ta make it hap - pen,＿＿＿

you got - ta make it hap -

1.

- pen.＿＿＿

2.

29

Verse 2:
Is it worth the aggravation
To find yourself a job
When there's nothing worth working for?
It's a crazy situation
But all I need
Are cigarettes and alcohol.

If You Tolerate This
Your Children Will Be Next

Words by Nicky Wire
Music by James Dean Bradfield & Sean Moore

© Copyright 1998 Sony/ATV Music Publishing (UK) Limited.
All Rights Reserved. International Copyright Secured.

Verse 2
Gravity keeps my head down
Or is it maybe shame
At being so young
And being so vain?
Holes in your head today
But I'm a pacifist,
I've walked La Ramblas
But with real intent.

And if you tolerate this etc.

Knockin' On Heaven's Door

Words & Music by Bob Dylan

© Copyright 1973 Ram's Horn Music, USA.
All Rights Reserved. International Copyright Secured.

I feel like I'm knock-in' on hea-ven's door.___
I feel like I'm knock-in on hea-ven's door.___

Knock, knock, knock-in' on hea-ven's door.___

Knock, knock, knock-in' on hea-ven's door.___

Waterloo Sunset

Words & Music by Ray Davies

© Copyright 1967 Davray Music Limited.
Carlin Music Corporation.
All Rights Reserved. International Copyright Secured.

Verse 2
Terry met Julie, Waterloo Station, every Friday night.
But I am so lazy, don't want to wander, I stay at home at night.
But I don't feel afraid.
As long as I gaze on Waterloo sunset I am in paradise.

Ev'ry day I look at the world *etc.*

Verse 3
Millions of people swarming like flies round Waterloo underground.
Terry and Julie lie cross over the river where they feel safe and sound.
And they don't need no friends.
As long as they gaze on Waterloo sunset they are in paradise.

Ev'ry day I look at the world *etc.*

Somebody Told Me

Words & Music by Brandon Flowers, Dave Keuning, Mark Stoermer & Ronnie Van Nucci

Original Key: B♭ minor

1. Break-ing my back just to know your name.__ Se-ven-teen tracks, and I've

© Copyright 2004 Universal Music Publishing Limited.
All Rights Reserved. International Copyright Secured.

place like this;__ I said - a hea - ven ain't close in a place like this.__

F   G   Am

Bring it back down, bring it back down to - night.__

F

Nev - er thought I'd let a ru - mour ru - in my__

Gsus⁴   N.C.   Am

__ moon - light.__ Well, some - bo - dy told__ me you had a boy -

46

friend who looked like a girl - friend that I had in Feb - ru - a - ry of last

year. It's not con - fi - den - tial. I've got po - ten - tial.

2. Rea- dy? Let's roll on-to some-thing new.___ Tak-ing it's toll, then I'm

leav -ing with - out you.___ 'Cos

48

Yellow

Words & Music by Guy Berryman, Jon Buckland, Will Champion & Chris Martin

Guitar Tuned:

① = D♯   ④ = B
② = B   ⑤ = A
③ = G   ⑥ = E

© Copyright 2000 BMG Music Publishing Limited.
All Rights Reserved. International Copyright Secured.

Verse 2:

I swam across, I jumped across for you.
Oh, what a thing to do.
'Cos you were all yellow,
I drew a line, I drew a line for you,
Oh, what a thing to do,
And it was all yellow.

Your skin, oh yeah, your skin and bones
Turn into something beautiful,
And you know, for you I'd bleed myself dry,
For you I'd bleed myself dry.

1 2 3 4 5 6 7 8 9

55

Bringing you the words and the music

All the latest music in print... rock & pop plus jazz, blues, country, classical and the best in West End show scores.

- Books to match your favourite CDs.

- Book-and-CD titles with high quality backing tracks for you to play along to. Now you can play guitar or piano with your favourite artist... or simply sing along!

- Audition songbooks with CD backing tracks for both male and female singers for all those with stars in their eyes.

- Can't read music? No problem, you can still play all the hits with our wide range of chord songbooks.

- Check out our range of instrumental tutorial titles, taking you from novice to expert in no time at all!

- Musical show scores include *The Phantom Of The Opera*, *Les Misérables*, *Mamma Mia* and many more hit productions.

- DVD master classes featuring the techniques of top artists.

Visit your local music shop or, in case of difficulty, contact the Marketing Department, Music Sales Limited, Newmarket Road, Bury St Edmunds, Suffolk, IP33 3YB, UK
marketing@musicsales.co.uk